IT'S MORE THAN *just a* COOKBOOK

ISBN 979-8-9867495-0-1

Contents

(42) Italian Blend

43	TURKEY ITALIAN PASTA
44	OMG SPAGHETTI
45	CHICKEN PARMESAN OVER ANGEL HAIR PASTA
46	THE BEST & EASIEST LASAGNA
47	ITALIAN TURKEY BURGER
48	ITALIAN BAKED CHICKEN

(55) MKTY Blend

56	TURKEY SALISBURY STEAK & GRAVY
57	TURKEY MEATLOAF
58	SPICY CABBAGE
59	SUMMER SALAD
60	BIEROCKS
61	CHICKEN CACCIATORE

(67) Pork Blend

68	STUFFED MUSHROOMS & STUFFED JALAPENOS
69	BRUSSEL SPROUT, BACON & ONIONS
70	PORK FRIED RICE
71	TERIYAKI PORK CHOPS
72	PORK TENDERLOIN

(81) Steak Blend

82	PERFECT STEAK
83	SIRLOIN CHEESEBURGER
84	TENDER ROAST BEEF
85	STEAK & BROCCOLI
86	NOT YOUR ORDINARY "ASPARAGUS"
87	TENDER BEEF TIPS & GRAVY

(49) Lemon Garlic Pepper Blend

50	LEMON PEPPER SALMON
51	CHICKEN ADOBO
52	LEMON BUTTER CHICKEN PASTA
53	LEMON PEPPER GARLIC WINGS
54	HONEY GARLIC CHICKEN WINGS

(62) Perfect Salt & Pepper Blend

63	CORNBREAD CASSEROLE
64	COLD PLATE
65	POTATO SALAD
66	EGGS OVER STEAK & POTATOES

(73) Spicy Blend

74	SPICY CHICKEN SANDWICH
75	SPICY BLACKEN SALMON
76	SPICY CHICKEN GOULASH
77	SPICY POTATOES
78	SPICY FRIED CHICKEN/TENDERS
79	SPICY ASPARAGUS PASTA
80	SPICY PINEAPPLE STEAK

(88) Taco Blend

89	MEXICAN PIZZA
90	BEEF FAJITAS
91	CHICKEN TACOS
92	TURKEY ENCHILADAS
93	TACO SALAD
94	MKTY STREET TACOS
95	MY! MY! MY! TACO PIE
96	OMG! FISH TACOS

Information

Thank you for purchasing my cookbook!

I hope *It's More than Just a Cookbook* inspires you to cook more because of the simplicity of the recipes and the flavorful MKTY BLENDS. Let's enjoy cooking!

Please be sure to visit our website: www.MKTY.org to order special MKTY BLENDS, and enjoy twelve flavorful blends perfect for any recipe.

Also, follow MKTY (My Kitchen to Yours) on IG and TikTok @mktycooking
Stay tuned for more MKTY BLENDS, cookbooks and other super cool things coming soon!

CONTACT: info@MKTY.org for more information.

Thank you for purchasing *It's More than just a Cookbook* and MKTY BLENDS.

Keep your eyes out for the paperback copy of It's More than just a Cookbook coming soon!!

Acknowledgements

First and foremost, I would like to thank my immediate family. Hands-down, you all are the kindest, most loving, supportive people I know. You are the wind beneath my wings.

Starting with my amazing husband
Ores "Spoony" Johnson Jr. thank you for being by my side during my illness and thank you for pushing me to pursue my dreams and vision. I thank God everyday for you! I love you forever.

To my awesome children
Darius & Venessa, Jordan & Brianna, Alexyss
Thank you for your continued support and thank you for sampling all these recipes. Y'all are my biggest supporters and critics. I love you forever.

To my grand-babies
Zeke and Ava
Mimi loves you infinitely to the moon and back. I love you forever.

Special thanks to the many **family and friends** that prayed for me to bring this cookbook to fruition. And to my sponsors A.J, L.N and an anonymous supporter.

Last but not least
my editor, graphic designer, my consultant, my "won't let me quit" person, my cheerleader, my daughter and my friend. I love you forever.
Miss Alexyss Johnson

"Remember to *ALWAYS* spice up your own happiness"
~Denisa Johnson

Preface

I know what you are probably thinking, do I really need another cookbook? The answer is, yes! After picking up this book, you are going to be glad you did. Because this is more than just a cookbook.

COOKING MADE SIMPLE...
In this cookbook, you will find my recipes that I have mastered over the years. After being a chef for over 20 years, I realized I wanted to offer a non-complicated cookbook, for those who love to cook but can go without the long complex recipes. However, I am not only sharing the recipes but also the special spices that truly elevate the recipe. I am so excited to introduce MKTY BLENDS.

My hope is that you will never have to worry or stress about how a recipe is going to taste or turn out ever again. With my one blend per recipe concept, it makes cooking easy and enjoyable!

Each blend (with the exception of the Perfect Salt & Pepper Blend) is prepared with low amounts of sodium. According to the American Heart Association, it is recommended to consume no more than 1500 mg of salt per day. That is why these blends are intentionally crafted with less salt, but if you would like to add more, just a few shakes of my Perfect Salt & Pepper Blend will do the trick! MKTY also offers the blends with no salt added.

After asking clients what their main concern was, most voiced that not knowing what spices or seasonings to use is what keeps them from attempting to cook other foods. Worry no more, I have found the solution to confident cooking, and I'm sharing it with you in this cookbook.

With MKTY BLENDS, no more grabbing five to six different spices and seasonings for one recipe. No more cluttered cabinets full of seasonings and spices. No more trying to figure out what seasonings taste better on chicken, beef, pork or seafood.

I have taken care of all these concerns for you!

This cookbook is like no other. The recipes are so straight forward, it is as easy as 1,2,3,4! I mean literally, most recipes have no more than four steps to each recipe. This helps you save time in the kitchen and allows you to enjoy cooking more instead of spending time reading lengthy, complex recipes.

These recipes are so easy that even a five year old can follow along, but the flavor is that of an experienced chef all because of MKTY BLENDS.

Want to know a secret? It is not a recipe that makes the food so delicious, it is the seasonings that give food its great taste!

Here you will find many recipes from all over to choose from. You have Asian, Mexican, American, Italian, and a wide variety of vegetarian dishes to choose from. Whatever your palate is craving, you can find it here.

Introduction

One day I went to prepare dinner and after five minutes of going through my cabinets looking for the ginger for my Asian Chicken Wings with an Orange Ginger Sauce, I became extremely frustrated moving around twenty five spices just to find the ginger suffocating in the back of the cabinet.

Right then and there is when I realized, why would I or anyone else in their right mind want to go on a scavenger hunt in their own cabinets, looking for five to six different spices, just to make one incredible dish? After finding all the spices I needed for that one recipe, I decided to blend my delicious MKTY Asian Blend that very night. I never wanted to worry about hunting for spices again, so I began to mix my special blends for other recipes as well.

While out of the kitchen due to recovering from a procedure, my clients were saying things like, "I wish we could clone you." "I wish we could buy your recipes!" "Can you prepare meals for us and can we pick them up?" I wanted to help out, but I was entirely too ill to honor their requests.

However, I decided to share my recipes and MKTY BLENDS with a few clients, which changed their lives for the better.

The concept behind It's More Than Just a Cookbook is for you to enjoy the simplicity of the recipes, significantly reduce the number of spices needed per dish, and to help eliminate the clutter from your spice cabinet. That is why you must purchase the MKTY BLENDS in order to get the full experience of It's More Than Just a Cookbook!

When this cookbook was just an idea, I had you in mind. I wanted to alleviate the stress of following complex recipes that take hours prepping, preparing and trying to figure out what spices to use for the best taste. That is why my MKTY BLENDS are deliciously flavored and paired to each recipe.

My culinary skills began at a very young age. My aunt would babysit me while my mother was at work and she would be in the kitchen from morning to night cooking all kinds of amazing dishes and guess who was her taste tester? You got it! It was me, taking it all in.

My first job was Head Cook at a senior citizen center, preparing lunch for 1500 seniors per day. Then I moved on to becoming the Dining Service Coordinator at an upscale assisted living facility, where I began my culinary experience in fine dining. Here I found my passion for cooking and catering which has grown into my very own personal chef business. After many years of cooking, I figured out the importance of consistency in the flavor of a dish through seasonings.

I always tell people it is not the recipe that gives you the flavor, it is the seasonings and spices. That is why I have decided to share my MKTY BLENDS with the world.

Each MKTY BLEND is carefully prepared with the best of ingredients, filled on demand for the freshest and boldest flavors. They come in six ounce, glass jars beautifully labeled with engraved bamboo lids, that are airtight to lock in the freshness of the Blends. All the spices are deliciously made with you in mind, we also offer "No Salt Added" options as well.

MKTY
ASIAN BLEND

This Asian Blend will bring a bright delightfulness into your food and kitchen. You are going to love it.

ASIAN CHICKEN WINGS
TOSSED IN ORANGE
GINGER SAUCE

SERVE WITH PORK FRIED RICE

4 SERVINGS   45 MINUTES

INGREDIENTS

4 lbs Chicken Wings

4 Tbsp Vegetable Oil

3 Tbsp **MKTY ASIAN BLEND**

ORANGE GINGER SAUCE

1 Cup Orange Juice

2 Tbsp Soy Sauce

2 Tbsp Ketchup

2 Tbsp Honey

2 Tbsp Cornstarch

1 Tbsp **MKTY ASIAN BLEND**

Chili flakes to taste

DIRECTIONS

PREHEAT OVEN TO 350°

1. Orange Ginger Sauce: Combine all the ingredients together in a saucepan and cook on low, continue to stir until thickened.
2. In a bowl, add oil, chicken wings, and MKTY Asian Blend and mix together. Place wings on a baking sheet and bake at 350° for 45 minutes.
3. Toss cooked wings into sauce. Enjoy!

Or use the air fryer: add a few chicken wings at a time for 12 minutes minutes on 350° and then flip and cook for an additional 12 minutes more.

SPRING ROLLS AND CHILI SAUCE

4 SERVINGS   45 MINUTES

INGREDIENTS

1 lbs Ground Pork*

16 oz bags of Coleslaw Mix (with cabbage and carrots)

8 Garlic (crushed)

2 Tbsp **MKTY ASIAN BLEND**

2 Tbsp Low Sodium Soy Sauce

1 Cup Vegetable Oil

1 Package Vietnamese Spring Roll Wrappers (25 sheets)

CHILI SAUCE

2 Cups Tomato Sauce

1/2 Cup Light Brown Sugar

1/4 Cup Red Wine Vinegar

2 tsp **MKTY ASIAN BLEND**

DIRECTIONS

1. Chili Sauce: In a saucepan combine all the ingredients together and cook on low, continue to stir until thickened. Serve with Spring Rolls

2. In a skillet add ground pork, garlic, soy sauce and MKTY Asian Blend. Cook until the meat is golden brown and add coleslaw and cook for 5 minutes longer. Drain and set aside too cool.

3. Separate each spring roll sheet and fill with 1 Tbsp of the meat mixture and roll. (Follow the directions on the package on how to roll.)

4. Heat oil in a skillet and add three to four Spring rolls at a time and cook until golden brown for about 3 minutes on each side. Enjoy!

*Can substitute for ground beef, chicken or turkey

PORK **STIR-FRY**

SERVE OVER SPAGHETTI NOODLES
OR RICE

4 SERVINGS   30 MINUTES

INGREDIENTS

4 Pork Chops*
2 Tbsp Olive Oil
1 Stalk of Broccoli (cut up)
1 Small bag of Sliced carrots
1 Small bag of Snow Peas
1 Small Onion (cut up)
1 Orange Bell Pepper (julienne cut)
4 Garlic Cloves
2 Tbsp **MKTY ASIAN BLEND**
1 Can Pineapple Chunks

SAUCE
1/2 Cup of Water
1/2 Cup Juice from the Pineapple
1/2 Cup Soy Sauce
2 tsp **MKTY PORK BLEND**
1 Tbsp Cornstarch

DIRECTIONS

1. <u>Sauce:</u> Mix water, pineapple juice, soy sauce, brown sugar, ginger, MKTY Pork Blend and Cornstarch in a small saucepan. Cook on low until thickened. Add to the meat and vegetables and serve over rice or noodles.
2. Rinse pork chops, pat dry with a paper towel, and season with MKTY Asian Blend. Sear in a hot skillet for 10 minutes on each side. Remove and cut horizontally.
3. In the same skillet sauté broccoli, carrots, bell peppers, onions and garlic until soft and translucent, add snow peas and pork the last 5 minutes (DO NOT OVERCOOK VEGETABLES). Enjoy!

Can be substituted for chicken or steak

PEPPER **STEAK**

SERVE OVER WHITE RICE

4 SERVINGS   30 MINUTES

INGREDIENTS

2 lbs Flank Steak (cut up)
1 Tbsp **MKTY ASIAN BLEND**
2 Tbsp Olive Oil
1 Red Bell Pepper (chunks)
1 Green Bell Peppers (chunks)
1 Small Yellow Onion (chunks)
5 Garlic Cloves (crushed)

SAUCE
1/4 Cup Brown Sugar
1/2 Cup Low Sodium Soy Sauce
2 tsp Sesame Seed Oil
2 tsp **MKTY ASIAN BLEND**
1 Tbsp Sriracha Sauce
1/4 Cup Water
1 Tbsp Cornstarch

DIRECTIONS

1. Sauce: In a saucepan mix brown sugar, soy sauce, sesame oil, MKTY Asian Blend, sriracha, water and cornstarch. Cook on low until thickened.

2. In a skillet gently sauté bell peppers and Onions in oil. And remove from the skillet.

3. In the same skillet add oil and sear seasoned cut up Flanks for 7 minutes on each side. Add the vegetables, sauce and the crushed garlic in with the meat and simmer for 2-3 minutes and Enjoy!

ASIAN CHICKEN SALAD

SERVE AS A MEAL

4 SERVINGS   15-45 MINUTES

INGREDIENTS

1 Whole Chicken or Rotisserie
Chicken from the Deli.
2 Tbsp **MKTY ASIAN BLEND**
1 Head Romaine Lettuce
1/2 Cup Cilantro (finely
chopped)
1 Can La Choy Chow Mein
Noodles

DRESSING

1 Cup Sesame Seed Oil
1/2 Cup Rice Vinegar
1/4 Cup Soy Sauce
4 Garlic (chopped)
2 Tbsp Sugar (optional)
1 Tbsp **MKTY ASIAN BLEND**

DIRECTIONS

1. Dressing: Prepare dressing by blending all the
   ingredients together in a jar and marinade in the
   refrigerator for an hour.
2. Shred lettuce and chop cilantro and mix together
   and set aside. **(If you purchased chicken from the
   Deli, skip STEP 3)**
3. Season the entire chicken with MKTY Asian Blend
   and bake for 45 minutes.
4. Pull chicken from the bone and shred. Serve
   chicken over lettuce mix, add noodles, and drizzle
   with Dressing. Enjoy!

TERIYAKI **SALMON**

SERVE WITH WHITE RICE AND
BROCCOLI & CARROT MIX

4 SERVINGS   30 MINUTES

INGREDIENTS

1 Slab King Salmon

1 Tbsp **MKTY ASIAN BLEND**

2 Tbsp Olive Oil

1 Bunch Green Onions

TERIYAKI SAUCE

1/2 Cup Soy Sauce

2 Tbsp Brown Sugar

2 Tbsp Water

1 Tbsp **MKTY ASIAN BLEND**

DIRECTIONS

1. Teriyaki Sauce: In a saucepan combine all the ingredients and cook slowly and stir constantly until thickened

2. Slice and season salmon with MKTY Asian Blend and grill in a hot skillet on both sides for 5 to 7 minutes until no longer pink or translucent.

3. Garnish salmon with teriyaki sauce and green onions. Enjoy!

LETTUCE **WRAPS**

4 SERVINGS   30 MINUTES

INGREDIENTS

1 lb Ground Turkey*
1 Package of Coleslaw Mix
1 Bunch Green Onions
(chopped)
2 Can Water Chestnuts
(chopped)
2 Tbsp **MKTY ASIAN BLEND**
2 Heads Butter Lettuce

SAUCE
2 Tbsp Butter
1/2 Cup Honey
1 Tbsp Soy Sauce
3 Garlic Cloves (crushed)
1 tsp **MKTY ASIAN BLEND**

DIRECTIONS

1. Sauce: In a saucepan mix all ingredients together and cook on low and continue to whisk.
2. In a skillet, brown ground turkey and season with MKTY Asian Blend. Add coleslaw, water chestnuts, green onions the last 5 minutes. and add the sauce.
3. Peel apart the lettuce and wash thoroughly.
4. Begin to fill each leaf with a tablespoon of meat. Enjoy!

*Can be substituted with ground beef or chicken.

19

MKTY
BARBECUE BLEND

Oh! My! Word! The aroma this blend sends off will have the entire neighborhood thinking you have a barbeque pit inside your home. You are going to love it.

HONEY BAKED **BARBECUE CHICKEN WINGS**

SERVE WITH GARLIC
MASHED POTATOES

4 SERVINGS   45 MINUTES

INGREDIENTS

4 lbs Chicken Wings*
4 Tbsp Vegetable Oil
3 Tbsp **MKTY BARBECUE BLEND**

HONEY BARBECUE SAUCE
2 Cups Ketchup
2 Tbsp **MKTY BARBECUE BLEND**
4 Tbsp Honey

DIRECTIONS

PREHEAT OVEN TO 350°

1. HONEY BARBECUE SAUCE: In a small saucepan combine ketchup and MKTY Barbecue Blend. Cook on low for 20 minutes and stir constantly. Be careful not to BURN! Base wings with sauce.

2. In a bowl, add oil and chicken wings. Place chicken wings on a baking sheet and season with MKTY Barbecue Blend. Bake at 350° for 45 minutes base the wings with barbecue sauce. Enjoy!

Or use the air fryer: Add a few chicken wings at a time for 12 minutes minutes on 350° and then flip and cook for an additional 12 minutes more.

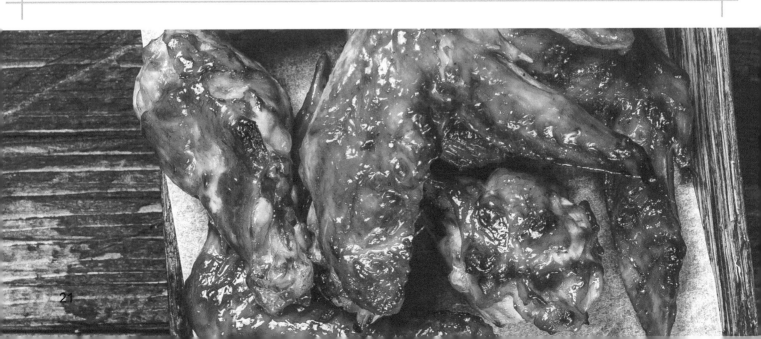

BARBECUE **STEAK**

SERVE WITH BAKED POTATO & NOT
YOUR ORDINARY ASPARAGUS

4 SERVINGS   30 MINUTES

INGREDIENTS

2 lbs Ribeye Steak
2 Tbsp **MKTY BARBECUE
BLEND**
4 Tbsp Butter

DIRECTIONS

1. Season steak with MKTY Barbecue Blend and add
   butter and steak to a hot cast-iron skillet. Sear steak
   on both sides for 5 to 6 minutes each.

*Remember it's not the recipe, it's the seasoning that makes
the flavor. Enjoy!*

BARBECUE **TURKEY WINGS**

SERVE WITH POTATO SALAD

4 SERVINGS   120 MINUTES

INGREDIENTS

4 Turkey Wings (can be cut in half)

1/2 Cup Oil

2 Tbsp **MKTY BARBECUE BLEND**

*Barbecue Sauce recipe is on page 25

DIRECTIONS

PREHEAT OVEN TO 350°

1. Season turkey wings with MKTY Barbecue Blend and place in a baking pan and cover tightly with foil.
2. Bake wings for 1 hour at 350°. After an hour, uncover wings and base them with MKTY barbecue sauce every 10 minutes until turkey wings are tender. Place under broiler for 5 minutes to get the charbroil look. Enjoy!

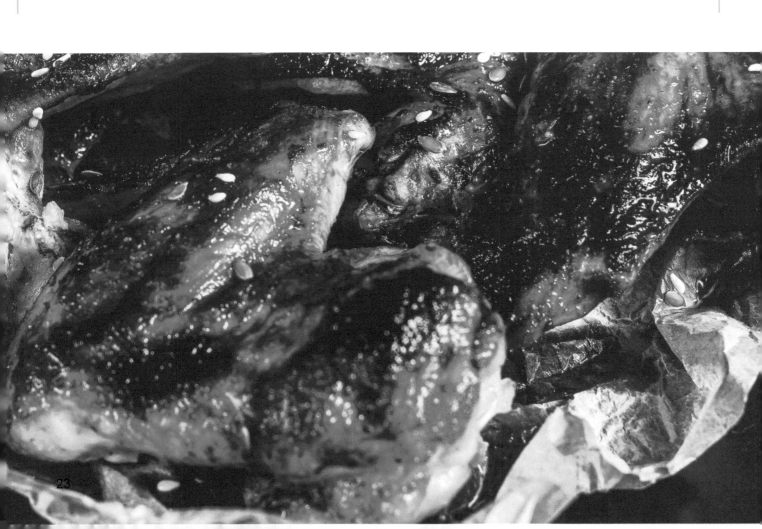

OVEN-BAKED
BARBECUE RIBS

SERVE WITH POTATO SALAD

4 SERVINGS   150 MINUTES

INGREDIENTS

1 Slab Baby Back Ribs
2 Tbsp **MKTY BARBECUE BLEND**

*Barbecue Sauce recipe is on page 25

DIRECTIONS

PREHEAT OVEN TO 350°

1. Rinse ribs and season with MKTY Barbecue Blend.
2. Place ribs on a baking sheet and bake at 350° for the first hour and turn over and cook for an additional hour. Base with barbecue sauce for the last 5 minutes and put the oven on Broil for the charbroil look.
3. Remove from the oven, let cool and slice. Enjoy!

BARBECUE SAUCE

4 SERVINGS   20 MINUTES

INGREDIENTS

2 Cup Ketchup
4 Tbsp Light Brown Sugar
(optional)
2 Tbsp **MKTY BARBECUE
BLEND**
1 Tbsp Worcestershire Sauce
1 tsp Chili Flakes

DIRECTIONS

1. In a saucepan, mix all the ingredients together and cook on low heat for 15 minutes. Enjoy!

MKTY
CAJUN BLEND

The way that this blend blackens your food is absolutely, amazingly, beautiful! It is heavy on the flavor, light on the spice. You are going to love it.

BLACKENED SHRIMP OVER ANGEL HAIR PASTA

4 SERVINGS   30 MINUTES

INGREDIENTS

2 lbs Shrimp (deveined)

1 lb Angel Hair Pasta (cook according to package)

1 Basket Cherry Tomatoes

1 Bag Spinach

6 Garlic Cloves

1 Fresh Parsley

1/2 Stick of Butter

1 Tbsp **MKTY CAJUN BLEND**

1 Tbsp Olive Oil

DIRECTIONS

1. Bring water to a boil, and cook pasta (according to the package), until al dente. Drain noodles, stir in 1 tbsp olive oil and set aside.
2. In a skillet, add 2 tbsp butter, shrimp, minced garlic and cook until shrimp becomes blackened, and remove.
3. In the same pan, add remaining 2 tbsp of butter, tomatoes, MKTY Cajun Blend, and sauté until tomatoes are soft, not mushy, then add spinach. Cook for an additional 2 minutes.
4. Add cooked pasta to tomatoes and spinach add shrimp, sprinkle with fresh parsley. Enjoy!

CRAB CAKES

4 SERVINGS   30 MINUTES

INGREDIENTS

3 Cans Crab Meat (chopped and drained)
1 Cup Onion (chopped)
1/2 Cup Red Bell Pepper (chopped)
1 Tbsp Olive oil
2 Eggs
1/2 Cup Mayonnaise
1 Tbsp Worcestershire Sauce
1 Tbsp **MKTY CAJUN BLEND**
1/4 Cup Fresh Parsley (chopped)
1 Cup Panko Bread Crumbs

LEMON ZEST SAUCE
1/2 Cup Mayonnaise
1 tsp Lemon Zest
2 Tbsp Lemon Juice
1 Pressed Garlic Clove

DIRECTIONS

1. Lemon Zest Sauce: In a small bowl, mix all the ingredients together and refrigerate.

2. In a non-stick pan, sauté finely chopped onions and bell peppers. Remove, drain and add to bowl.

3. In a bowl, mix eggs, mayonnaise, Worcestershire, MKTY Cajun Blend, Panko bread crumbs, fresh parsley, crab meat and sautéed vegetables. Scoop mixture into your hands and form 12 small patties.

4. In a non-stick pan, add oil and fry patties for 4 to 5 minutes on each side, twice or until golden brown. Enjoy!

BLACKENED SHRIMP
SALAD

SERVE AS AN ENTREE

4 SERVINGS   30 MINUTES

INGREDIENTS

2 lbs Fresh Shrimp (deveined)
1/2 Cup Buttermilk
3/4 Cup Cornstarch
1 Tbsp **MKTY CAJUN BLEND**
4 Tbsp Butter
1 Head of Butter Leaf Lettuce
(shredded)
1 Bunch of Cilantro (chopped)

SAUCE
1 Cup Mayonnaise
1/2 Cup Sriracha
2 tsp **MKTY ASIAN BLEND**
1/4 Cup Rice Vinegar
1/4 Cup Honey

DIRECTIONS

1. SAUCE: In a medium bowl mix all ingredients together and refrigerate.
2. Mix cornstarch with MKTY Cajun Blend. Add shrimp to buttermilk. Dredge each shrimp in cornstarch and shake excess.
3. In a skillet, melt butter on medium heat and add 6 to 8 seasoned shrimps at a time. Blacken shrimp on both sides until the color is pink. Remove shrimp and serve over a bed of lettuce mixed with cilantro and drizzle with sauce. Enjoy!

BLACKENED SALMON

SERVE WITH "NOT YOUR ORDINARY ASPARAGUS" AND MASHED POTATOES

4 SERVINGS   30 MINUTES

INGREDIENTS
1 Slab Salmon
2 Tbsp **MKTY CAJUN BLEND**
2 Tbsp Olive Oil
1/4 Cup Cilantro

DIRECTIONS
1. Rinse and cut in fours. Season salmon on both sides with MKTY Cajun Blend.
2. In a skillet, heat oil and blacken salmon on each side for 5 to 7 minutes or until no longer translucent pink.
3. Garnish with fresh cilantro. Enjoy!

BLACKENED **CHICKEN**

SERVE WITH CHICKEN FLAVORED
RICE AND BRUSSEL SPROUTS, BACON
& ONIONS

4 SERVINGS   30 MINUTES

INGREDIENTS
4 lbs Chicken Wings*
2 Tbsp **MKTY CAJUN BLEND**
4 Tbsp Olive Oil
sprinkle chili flakes

DIRECTIONS
1. In a bowl, add oil and season chicken on both sides with MKTY Cajun Blend.
2. Heat skillet on medium-heat and blacken chicken on each side for 7 to 10 minutes, twice or until fully cooked on the inside.

Or add chicken to the air fryer for 20 minutes minutes at 380° and then flip and cook for an additional 15 minutes more. Enjoy!

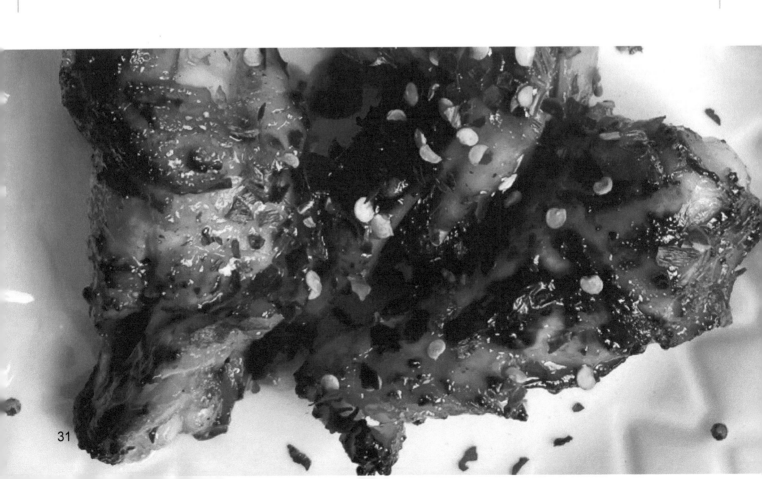

MKTY
CHICKEN BLEND

This Chicken Blend has all the right flavors to make your taste buds leap with joy. You are going to love it.

BACON MAC-N-CHEESE

SERVE AS A SIDE OR
MAIN DISH

4 SERVINGS   30 MINUTES

INGREDIENTS
1/2 lb Bacon
1/2 Box of Elbow Macaroni

CHEESE SAUCE
4 Tbsp Butter
4 Tbsp Flour
3 Cups Cheddar Cheese
2 Cups Milk
2 Tbsp **MKTY CHICKEN BLEND**

DIRECTIONS
1. Cheese Sauce: In a pot, melt butter add flour and whisk in milk until smooth and thick, add cheese and cook on low, continue to whisk until cheese is melted.
2. In a pot, boil pasta according to the package and drain water.
3. In a skillet, fry bacon to a crisp and chop it into small pieces.
4. In a bowl, pour cheese sauce over pasta, add bacon and season with MKTY Chicken Blend. Enjoy!

SWEET POTATO TACOS

4 SERVINGS   30 MINUTES

INGREDIENTS
3 Large Sweet Potatoes (diced)
1 Bag of Spinach
2 Tbsp Butter
1 Tbsp **MKTY CHICKEN BLEND**
12 Corn Tortillas

SALSA
3 Tomatoes
1 Cilantro
1 16 oz Black Beans (drained)
1 Onion (diced)
1 Jalapeno (seedless)
1 Lime
2 Avocado (sliced)

DIRECTIONS
1. Salsa: In a bowl, mix diced tomatoes, diced onions, chopped cilantro, black beans, chopped jalapeno, MKTY Chicken Blend and squeezed lime juice. Toss until perfectly mixed. Add a pinch of MKTY Salt & Pepper
2. In a pan, saute diced sweet potatoes in butter and cook until tender. Add spinach and season with MKTY Chicken Blend.
3. Lightly fry tortilla shells and fill with potato mixture. Top with salsa and sliced avocado. Enjoy!

CHICKEN FLAVORED **FRIED RICE**

**SERVE WITH PORK CHOPS &
NOT YOUR ORDINARY
ASPARAGUS**

4 SERVINGS   30 MINUTES

INGREDIENTS

2 Cups Rice

3 Cups Water

3 Tbsp **MKTY CHICKEN BLEND**

1/2 Stick Butter

1/2 Yellow Onion

DIRECTIONS

1. In a cast iron skillet, brown the rice and onions in butter until rice is a golden color, and add water and MKTY Chicken Blend. Cover with lid and cook on low for 30 minutes. Let cool 10 minutes.

2. Fluff Rice with fork and Enjoy!

Optional: Fried bacon and green onions can be added at the end.

CAULIFLOWER STEAK

4 SERVINGS   30 MINUTES

INGREDIENTS

2 Head of Cauliflower
4 Tbsp Olive Oil
2 Tbsp **MKTY CHICKEN BLEND**

DIRECTIONS

1. Slice cauliflower from top to bottom 2" thick. Season with MKTY Chicken Blend.
2. Heat the skillet on medium and add oil.
3. Grill cauliflower for 5 to 6 minutes per side until golden brown. Enjoy!

OH! **CHICKEN WINGS**

SERVE WITH OVEN BAKED
POTATO WEDGES

4 SERVINGS   45 MINUTES

INGREDIENTS

4 lbs Chicken wings*
3 Tbsp Vegetable Oil
2 Tbsp **MKTY CHICKEN BLEND**

SAUCE
2 Tbsp Butter
1 Cup Honey
3 Garlic cloves (crushed)

DIRECTIONS

PREHEAT OVEN TO 350°

1. SAUCE: In a saucepan heat butter, honey and crushed garlic until thickened (be careful not to burn).
2. On a baking sheet base chicken with oil and season chicken wings with MKTY Chicken Blend. Bake at 350 degrees for 45 minutes.
3. Toss the wings in the sauce and place the wings back in the oven for 5 minutes. Enjoy!

Or use the air fryer: add a few chicken wings at a time for 12 minutes minutes on 350° and then flip and cook for an additional 12 minutes more.

LOADED POTATO WITH GROUND TURKEY, SPINACH AND CHEESE

SERVE WITH GARDEN SALAD

4 SERVINGS   45 MINUTES

INGREDIENTS

1/2 lb Ground Turkey*
4 Large Potatoes
Oil For Each Potato
1 Tbsp **MKTY CHICKEN BLEND**
1 Bag of Spinach
8 oz Mozzarella Cheese (shredded)
Black Bean & Corn Salsa
Sour Cream (optional)

DIRECTIONS

PREHEAT OVEN TO 350°

1. Wrap oiled potato in foil and bake at 350 degrees for 45 minutes or until soft.
2. In a pan brown ground turkey and season with MKTY Chicken Blend. When meat is brown, add spinach and cook for 1 minute longer.
3. Stuff potato with meat, cheese, salsa and sour cream. Enjoy!

*Can substitute for ground beef or Impossible meat.

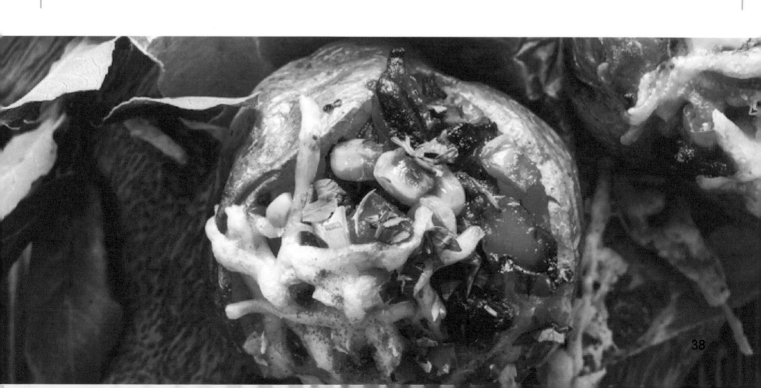

38

CHICKEN ALFREDO

SERVE WITH A GARDEN SALAD

4 SERVINGS   30 MINUTES

INGREDIENTS

1 Small pack Fettuccine (follow package directions)
4 Chicken Breast (cut boneless breast into chunks)
2 Tbsp **MKTY CHICKEN BLEND**
3 Tbsp Olive Oil

SAUCE
3 Tablespoons Butter
4 oz Cream Cheese (soften)
1 Cup Heavy Whipping Cream
2 Large Garlic Cloves
1 Cup Parmesan Cheese (Freshly Grated)
2 Tbsp **MKTY CHICKEN BLEND**

DIRECTIONS

1. Follow package instructions for cooking Fettuccine.
2. Sauce: In a skillet add the butter, cream cheese and whipping cream over low heat, stir occasionally until cheese melts into the sauce, cook until the sauce has reduced and stir in parmesan cheese until melted. Reduce heat and season with MKTY Chicken Blend. (If too thick add more heavy whipping cream)
3. In a skillet, add oil and seasoned chicken breast, blacken on both sides 5 to 7 minutes, twice or until no longer pink.
4. Toss the cooked pasta into the sauce and chunks of chicken .
5. Top with grilled chicken and add extra parmesan. Enjoy!

CHICKEN ENCHILADAS

SERVE WITH BEANS AND RICE

4 SERVINGS   45 MINUTES

INGREDIENTS

3 lbs Chicken thighs (boneless)
2 Cups Water
1 Cup Onion
3/4 Cup Bell pepper
8 Tomatillo
1/2 Sour Cream
2 Tbsp **MKTY CHICKEN BLEND**
2 Cups Mozzarella Cheese
12 Corn Tortillas
1/4 Cup Vegetable Oil

DIRECTIONS

PREHEAT OVEN TO 350°

1. In a medium size pot add water, onions, bell peppers, chicken thighs and MKTY Chicken Blend and cook for 30 minutes or until tender. DO NOT DISCARD THE BROTH Remove chicken from the pot and let cool and shred.
2. SAUCE: Add tomatillo to the chicken broth and cook until tender, add sour cream, broth and tomatillo into a blender, blend until smooth (this is your enchilada sauce).
3. In a skillet: add oil and Soften tortilla shells for 1 minute and then dip each shell in the enchilada sauce and fill each shell with meat and cheese and arrange in a 9 x 13 baking pan. Pour remaining sauce over the shells and sprinkle with cheese and green onions
4. Bake at 350 degrees for 20 minutes. Let them cool for 5 minutes. Enjoy!

VEGETABLE SOUP WITH IMPOSSIBLE SAUSAGE

SERVE WITH A GARDEN SALAD
AND ROLL

4 SERVINGS   30 MINUTES

INGREDIENTS

2-14 oz Impossible Sausage* (pull apart)

3-14.5 oz Cans of Chicken Broth

1 ½ Cups of Water

1/2 Head of Cauliflower (florets)

2 Cans of Sweet Corn (drained)

2 Tbsp **MKTY CHICKEN BLEND**

1 Yellow Squash (diced)

1 Zucchini (diced)

2-14 oz Diced Tomatoes

10 oz Bag of Spinach

DIRECTIONS

1. In a medium size pot add chicken broth, water, cauliflower, corn, MKTY Chicken Blend and add pieces of sausage. Cook for 15 minutes,

2. Now add tomatoes, squash and zucchini and cook for an additional 10 minutes before adding the spinach, stir well and taste to see if more seasoning is needed. Enjoy!

This recipe is so fun because you can use any sort of vegetables you choose to use. And meat can be substituted for ground turkey, ground beef or chopped chicken.

MKTY
ITALIAN BLEND

This is no ordinary Italian seasoning. The added garlic kicks it up a few notches. You are going to love it.

TURKEY ITALIAN PASTA

4 SERVINGS   30 MINUTES

INGREDIENTS

1 ½ lbs Ground Turkey*

2 Tbsp **MKTY ITALIAN BLEND**

2 Cup Mushrooms (sliced)

1/2 Cup Onion (chopped)

1/2 Cup Red Bell Peppers (chopped)

1 Box of Cavatelli (follow instructions on the box)

SAUCE

4 Tbsp Butter

4 Tbsp Flour

2 Cups Heavy Cream

2 Tbsp Cornstarch

2 Cups Parmesan Cheese (shredded)

1 tsp Crushed Chili Peppers (optional)

2 Tbsp **MKTY ITALIAN BLEND**

DIRECTIONS

1. Boil pasta according to the package.

2. Sauce: In a saucepan on low heat, melt butter and add flour, whisk until smooth. Then add heavy whipping cream, cornstarch, and the cheese, continue to whisk until smooth.

3. In a pan, add meat and vegetables, season with MKTY Italian Blend. Cook until the meat is brown.

4. Drain and mix sauce, meat and pasta. Enjoy!

Can substitute for ground beef, ground pork or chicken

OMG **SPAGHETTI**

4 SERVINGS   30 MINUTES

INGREDIENTS

1 lb Ground Turkey*
1/2 lb Kielbasa Sausage
1/2 Green Bell Pepper
1/2 Yellow Onion
1 lb Mushrooms
6 Garlic cloves (crushed)
2 Tbsp **MKTY ITALIAN BLEND**
1 Pack Thin Spaghetti Noodles

SAUCE
32 oz Tomato Sauce
8 oz Tomato Paste
16 oz Diced Tomatoes (drained)
2 Tbsp **MKTY ITALIAN BLEND**

DIRECTIONS

1. Sauce: In a saucepan simmer tomato sauce and diced tomatoes with MKTY Italian Blend on low for 30 minutes. (watch closely)
2. In a pot, boil spaghetti noodles according to the package.
3. In a skillet, season meat with MKTY Italian Blend and add onions, garlic and mushrooms. Cook until vegetables are translucent and meat is brown.
4. Drain spaghetti noodles, add the meat and the sauce to the spaghetti and mix well. Enjoy!

*Can substitute for ground beef or Impossible Meat

CHICKEN PARMESAN OVER ANGEL HAIR PASTA

SERVE WITH GREEN SALAD OR STEAMED BROCCOLI

4 SERVINGS   30 MINUTES

INGREDIENTS

4 Chicken Breast (skinless and boneless)
2 Tbsp Olive Oil
2 Eggs
1 Tbsp Water
2 Cups Panko Bread Crumbs
1 CUP Parmesan Cheese (grated)
3 Tbsp **MKTY ITALIAN BLEND**
4 slices Provolone Cheese
16 oz Spaghetti Sauce (favorite one) or homemade

SAUCE
16 oz Tomato Sauce
4 oz Tomato Paste
16 oz Diced Tomatoes (drained)
2 Tbsp **MKTY ITALIAN BLEND**

DIRECTIONS

1. Sauce: In a small pot, add all the ingredients together and simmer on low for 20 minutes.
2. In a bowl mix bread crumbs and parmesan cheese.
3. In another bowl mix 2 eggs and water mix well
4. Season chicken breast with MKTY Italian Blend, dip in egg, and then cover in bread crumbs.
5. In a skillet, add oil and fry chicken for 5 to 7 minutes on each side, twice or until golden brown and fully cooked on the inside.
6. Place Provolone cheese on top of chicken until melted. Add sauce to noodles and place chicken on top. Enjoy!

THE BEST & EASIEST
LASAGNA

SERVE WITH A GARDEN SALAD AND ROLL

4 SERVINGS   60 MINUTES

INGREDIENTS
1 lb Ground Beef*
1/2 lb Ground Sweet Italian Sausage
2 Tbsp **MKTY ITALIAN BLEND**
4 Garlic Cloves (crushed)
32 oz Ragu Spaghetti Sauce
15 oz Ricotta Cheese
3 Cups Mozzarella Cheese (shredded)
2 Eggs
3/4 Cups Parmesan (shredded)
2 tsp Dried Parsley
12 Lasagna Noodles (No Boil Noodles)
1/4 Cup Water

DIRECTIONS
PREHEAT OVEN TO 350°

1. In a pan brown both meats with garlic, onions, and MKTY Italian Blend. Drain and add Ragu sauce.
2. Mix in a bowl ricotta, mozzarella, eggs, parmesan cheese, and parsley. Set aside.
3. In a glass baking dish begin to layer with meat sauce on the bottom, then 3 noodles across the length of the pan, meat sauce, 3 noodles, cheese mixture, 3 noodles, meat sauce, 3 noodles, cheese mixture, 3 noodle and top with remaining meat and mozzarella cheese.
4. Add water to the pan and cover with foil. Bake at 350 degrees for 45 minutes to an hour. Uncover and lightly broil for the last 5 minutes. Be sure the noodles are soft before removing lasagna from the oven. Enjoy!

Can be substituted for ground turkey or Impossible Meat

ITALIAN **TURKEY BURGER**

SERVE WITH SWEET
POTATOES FRIES

8 SERVINGS   30 MINUTES

INGREDIENTS

1 lbs Ground Turkey*

1/2 lb Italian Sausage

3 Tbsp **MKTY ITALIAN BLEND**

1 Egg

1/2 Cup Onion (finely chopped)

2 Tbsp Olive Oil

2 Cups Panko Bread Crumbs

2 Provolone Cheese (slices)

1 Head of Lettuce

3 Tomatoes

8 Hamburger Buns

SAUCE

8 oz Tomato Sauce

4 oz Tomato Paste

1 Tbsp **MKTY ITALIAN BLEND**

DIRECTIONS

1. Sauce: In a small saucepan, mix all ingredients together and simmer for 20 minutes.
2. In a mixing bowl, combine ground turkey, Italian sausage, MKTY Italian Blend, egg, and onions and form small patties. Makes 8 patties
3. In a bowl, mix Panko bread crumbs and parmesan cheese. Roll patties into bread crumbs
4. In a skillet add oil and fry patties on medium heat, about 5 minutes on each side, twice.
5. Lightly butter buns and toast in a skillet for a nice crunch, then build your burger. Garnish with lettuce, tomato, cheese and dip the burger in sauce. Enjoy!

Can substitute for ground Beef or Impossible Meat

ITALIAN **BAKED CHICKEN**

SERVE WITH CHICKEN RICE
AND GREEN BEANS

4 SERVINGS   30 MINUTES

INGREDIENTS
8 Chicken Breast or Thighs
3 Tbsp **MKTY ITALIAN BLEND**
4 Tbsp Olive Oil

DIRECTIONS
PREHEAT OVEN TO 350°

1. Rinse and butterfly the chicken breast with a knife.
2. In a bowl, add oil, chicken and MKTY Italian Blend. Mix well.
3. On a baking sheet add seasoned chicken and bake at 350 degrees for 30 minutes. Enjoy!

Or use the air fryer: add chicken for 15 minutes minutes at 350° and then flip and cook for an additional 12 minutes more. Can use 4 lbs chiken wings

MKTY
LEMON GARLIC PEPPER BLEND

This flavor was elaborated on all levels when coming up with this blend. It is sure to make your mouth water for more. You are going to love it.

LEMON PEPPER **SALMON**

4 SERVINGS   30 MINUTES

INGREDIENTS

1 Slab Salmon
2 Tbsp Olive Oil
1 Tbsp **MKTY LEMON GARLIC PEPPER BLEND**

LEMON BUTTER SAUCE
4 Tbsp Butter
2 Tbsp Lemon Juice
1 Tbsp **MKTY LEMON GARLIC PEPPER BLEND**

DIRECTIONS

1. Lemon Butter Sauce: In a pot, add butter, lemon juice and MKTY Lemon Garlic Pepper Blend sprinkle to taste .
2. Brush olive oil on sliced salmon and season with MKTY Lemon Garlic Pepper Blend, place in a hot skillet and blacken for 5 to 7 minutes on both sides, twice or until no longer translucent. Remove from the skillet.
3. Pour sauce over cooked Salmon and Enjoy!

CHICKEN ADOBO

4 SERVINGS   30 MINUTES

INGREDIENTS

1 Package Chicken Thighs* (8-10 pieces)

4 Tbsp Vegetable oil

2 Cups Apple cider Vinegar

2 Cups Low Sodium Soy Sauce

4 Bay Leaves

8 Garlic Cloves

4 Tbsp **MKTY LEMON GARLIC PEPPER BLEND**

DIRECTIONS

1. Season chicken with MKTY Lemon Garlic Pepper Blend and sear chicken in a hot skillet with oil until golden brown.
2. Add seared chicken with all the other ingredients to a pot, cover and boil on medium heat for 40 minutes.
3. Serve immediately over rice and Enjoy!

Can be substituted for pork chops

LEMON BUTTER **CHICKEN PASTA**

SERVE WITH STEAMED BROCCOLI

4 SERVINGS   30 MINUTES

INGREDIENTS

2 Tbsp Flour

2 Tbsp **MKTY LEMON GARLIC PEPPER BLEND**

4 Tbsp Oil

1 Box of Rigatoni Noodles (cook according to package)

SAUCE

4 Tbsp Butter

4 Tbsp Lemon Juice

1 ½ Cup Chicken Broth

1/2 Cup Heavy Cream

1/3 Cup Parmesan Cheese (grated)

2 Tbsp **MKTY LEMON GARLIC PEPPER BLEND**

1 Tbsp Cornstarch

Pinch of Fresh Parsley

DIRECTIONS

1. Sauce: In a saucepan, melt the butter and sauté mushrooms and red bell peppers for 10 minutes, then add lemon juice, heavy cream, chicken broth, MKTY Lemon Garlic Pepper Blend and cornstarch whisk sauce until smooth, not runny.
2. Cook noodles according to the package.
3. In a bowl add flour and MKTY Lemon Garlic Pepper Blend. Dredge chicken in flour mixture and shake off excess.
4. Heat oil in a frying pan on medium heat and crisp chicken on each side for about 5 to 7 minutes on each side, twice or until no longer pink. Slice and Set aside.
5. Pour sauce over cooked Pasta and add sliced chicken breast on top. (Garnish with Parsley and Lemon slices.) Enjoy!

* Or use the air fryer: add chicken and spray with Pam cooking spray, fry for 15 minutes at 350° and then flip and cook for an additional 15 minutes more.

BAKED GARLIC LEMON PEPPER **WINGS**

SERVE WITH A GARDEN SALAD AND ROLL

4 SERVINGS   40 MINUTES

INGREDIENTS

4 lbs Chicken Wings*

4 Tbsp Vegetable Oil

3 Tbsp **MKTY LEMON GARLIC PEPPER BLEND**

DIRECTIONS

PREHEAT OVEN TO 350°

1. In a bowl, mix oil and the wings. Line them on a baking sheet and season with MKTY Lemon Garlic Pepper Blend.
2. Bake at 350 degrees for 40 minutes or until no longer pink.
3. Bake for an additional 5 minutes on broil to get the charbroil appearance. Enjoy!

Or use the air fryer: add a few chicken wings and spray with Pam cooking spray, fry for 15 minutes at 350° and then flip and cook for an additional 15 minutes more.

MKTY BLEND

All my favorite spices and seasoning blended together for a full blown explosion of deliciousness. You are absolutely going to love it.

HONEY GARLIC **CHICKEN WINGS**

SERVE WITH GARLIC ROASTED POTATOES

4 SERVINGS   45 MINUTES

INGREDIENTS

4 lbs Chicken Wings*
4 Tbsp Oil
2 Tbsp **MKTY LEMON GARLIC PEPPER BLEND**

SAUCE
2 Tbsp Butter
1 Cup Honey
6 Garlic Cloves (crushed)
1 Tbsp **MKTY LEMON GARLIC PEPPER BLEND**

DIRECTIONS

PREHEAT OVEN TO 350°

1. Sauce: In a saucepan, melt butter, add honey and MKTY Lemon Garlic Pepper Blend. Cook on low until thickened. (be careful not to BURN!)
2. In a bowl, add oil to chicken wings and season with MKTY Lemon Garlic Blend. Place wings on a baking sheet and bake at 350 degrees for 45 minutes.
3. Dip the wings into sauce immediately. Enjoy!

Or use the air fryer: add a few chicken wings and spray with Pam cooking spray, fry for 15 minutes at 350° and then flip and cook for an additional 15 minutes more.

55

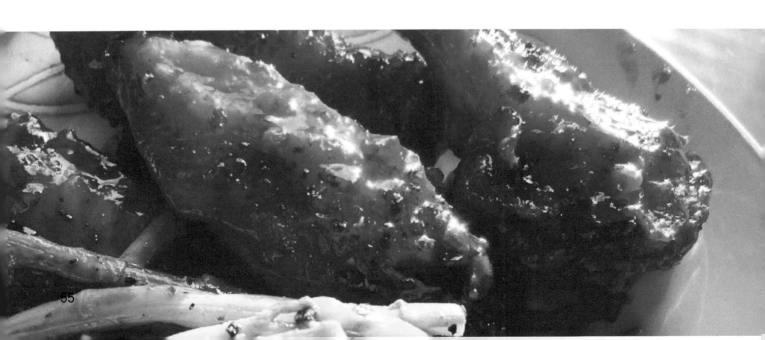

TURKEY SALISBURY STEAK & GRAVY

SERVE OVER WHIPPED MASHED POTATOES

4 SERVINGS   40 MINUTES

INGREDIENTS

1 lbs Ground Turkey*

3 Tbsp **MKTY BLEND**

2 Slices of Bread

1/4 Cup Milk

2 Eggs

Gravy

3 Tbsp Flour

3 Tbsp Vegetable Oil

16 oz Can Chicken Broth

2 Cups Mushrooms (sliced)

1 Cup Onion (julienne style)

DIRECTIONS

PREHEAT OVEN TO 350°

1. Soak bread in milk and set aside.
2. Gravy: In a small saucepan on medium heat, mix flour and oil until smooth, cook until golden brown. Add chicken broth and 1 Tbsp MKTY Blend, add onions and mushrooms and cook for 10 minutes.
3. In a large mixing bowl, add ground turkey, bread, eggs and season with MKTY Blend.
4. Form 8 medium-size patties and place in a glass baking pan. Bake at 350 degrees for 20 minutes and then add gravy to the baking pan and bake for an additional 15 minutes. Enjoy!

*Can be substituted for ground beef or Impossible Meat

TURKEY MEATLOAF

4 SERVINGS   45 MINUTES

INGREDIENTS

1 lb Ground Turkey*
1/2 Yellow Onion (finely diced)
4 Garlic (diced)
1/2 Red Bell Pepper (diced)
2 Tbsp Worcestershire Sauce
3 Tbsp **MKTY BLEND**
1/4 Cup Milk
2 Slices of White Bread
1 Egg

SAUCE
1 Cup Ketchup
2 Tbsp Light Brown Sugar
2 tsp Worcestershire Sauce

DIRECTIONS

PREHEAT OVEN TO 350°

1. Sauce: Mix ketchup, brown sugar and Worcestershire sauce together
2. Soak bread in milk and set aside.
3. In a large mixing bowl add ground turkey, bell peppers, onions, Worcestershire sauce, MKTY Blend, bread and eggs, and mix well.
4. Place in a loaf pan and bake at 350 degrees for 30 minutes. Base meatloaf with sauce for the last 10 minutes on broil to get the charbroiled look. Enjoy!

Can be substituted for ground beef or Impossible Meat

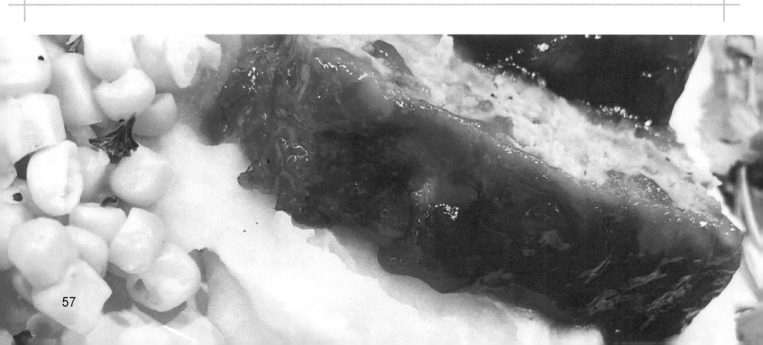

57

SPICY **CABBAGE**

SERVE AS A SIDE OR OVER RICE

4 SERVINGS   30 MINUTES

INGREDIENTS

2 Head Green Cabbage

4 Tbsp Butter

1/2 Red Bell Pepper

1/2 Green Bell Pepper

1 Small Onion

1 Jalapeño (without seeds)

1/2 Pack of Bacon

2 Tbsp Sugar

2 Tbsp Apple Cider Vinegar

1 Tbsp **MKTY BLEND**

DIRECTIONS

1. Chop cabbage into small squares, dice onions and chop and remove seeds from jalapeño.
2. In a pot, fry bacon, onions, bell peppers and jalapeño and cook until bacon is crisp, then add cabbage, sugar, vinegar and MKTY Blend.
3. Cover and cook for 20 minutes until cabbage is soft (not mushy). Enjoy!

It's not to spicy at all.

SUMMER **SALAD**

4 SERVINGS   30 MINUTES

INGREDIENTS

1 Ear of Corn
1/2 Cup Cherry Tomatoes
1/2 Cup Red Onion (diced)
1 Can Black Beans (optional)
1/2 Jalapeño (diced and optional)
1 Avocado (ripe)

DRESSING

1/4 Cup Lime Juice (fresh)
2 Garlic (chopped)
1/4 Cup Fresh Parsley (finely chopped)
2 tsp **MKTY BLEND**
2 Tbsp Olive Oil (extra virgin)

DIRECTIONS

1. Dressing: In a bowl, Whisk all the ingredients together and slowly drizzle in the olive oil while whisking. Set aside.

2. In a pot, boil the corn in salt and pepper water for 4 minutes or so, until tender. When cool, strip the kernels off the cob.

3. In a large bowl combine corn, tomatoes, black beans, red onion and jalapeños, add the avocados last to prevent mushiness. Toss with the dressing, salad is best served chilled. Enjoy!

BIEROCKS

SERVE WITH RICE PILAF AND
SALAD

4 SERVINGS   30 MINUTES

INGREDIENTS

1 lb Ground Turkey*
1 Large bag of Coleslaw with
Carrots
6 Garlic Cloves (chopped)
1/2 Small Onion (diced)
1 Cup Rice (cooked and cooled)
3 Tbsp **MKTY BLEND**
12 Frozen Dinner Rolls
2 Tbsp Butter

DIRECTIONS

PREHEAT OVEN TO 350°

1. Cook rice ahead of time to be sure it's cool to handle.
2. Place rolls on a baking sheet and let them rise according to the package. While the rolls are rising:
3. In a skillet, brown seasoned ground turkey with MKTY Blend, add vegetables and cook until vegetables are soft. Drain mixture and set aside. Add cool rice to meat and vegetables.
4. Carefully, pull on the dinner roll and flatten it out and fill with 1 Tbsp of the meat mixture and cheese. Begin to close the roll around the filling.
5. Place filled roll on a buttered baking sheet and bake at 350 degrees for 20 minutes or until golden brown. Dust with melted butter and Enjoy!!

CHICKEN CACCIATORE

4 SERVINGS   30 MINUTES

INGREDIENTS

4 Chicken Breast (slice in halves)

2 Tbsp **MKTY BLEND**

1/2 Cup Onion (cut julienne style)

1/2 Green Bell Pepper (cut julienne style)

4 Garlic Cloves (finely chopped)

2 Cups Mushrooms (sliced)

8 oz Can of Black Olives (drained and optional)

SAUCE

16 oz Tomato Sauce

8 oz Tomato Paste

1 Tbsp **MKTY ITALIAN BLEND**

DIRECTIONS

PREHEAT OVEN TO 350°

1. SAUCE: In a small saucepan, combine all ingredients together and simmer for 20 minutes and set aside.

2. In a skillet season chicken breast with MKTY Blend and blacken in olive oil for 5 TO 7 minutes on each side. Remove and place in a baking dish.

3. Add onions and bell peppers to the pan and sauté, add garlic, mushrooms and sauce.

4. Pour over chicken breast and bake at 350 degrees for 20 minutes. Enjoy!

61

MKTY
PERFECT SALT AND PEPPER BLEND

The right amount of salt and pepper, with a touch of parsley for color and flavor. You are going to love it.

CORNBREAD CASSEROLE

4 SERVINGS   40 MINUTES

INGREDIENTS

2 Cans Sweet Corn (drained)
1 Cup Yellow Onion (chopped)
4 Tbsp Butter
2 Box Jiffy Cornbread Mix
1 Cup Sour Cream
1 Cup Cheddar Cheese
1/2 Tbsp **MKTY PERFECT S&P BLEND**
3 Tbsp Vegetable Oil

DIRECTIONS

PREHEAT OVEN TO 350°

1. Sauté chopped onions in butter.
2. In a mixing bowl prepare Jiffy according to directions (DO NOT BAKE YET.) Add onions, sour cream, cheese, and MKTY S&P Blend to the Jiffy mix.
3. Pour mixture in a greased cast iron skillet. Bake at 350° for 40 minutes. Enjoy!

COLD PLATE

4 SERVINGS   30 MINUTES

INGREDIENTS

Pea Salad- Use two cans of sweet
Peas (drained)
Tuna Salad- Use two cans of tuna
(drained)
Macaroni Salad- Cook macaroni
according to package

2 Eggs (boiled)
3 Cups
1/2 Yellow Onion (diced small)
1/4 Cup Sweet Relish
1/2 Cup Mayonnaise
1 tsp **MKTY PERFECT S&P
BLEND**
1 Tbsp Vinegar
1 Tbsp Sugar

DIRECTIONS

1. In a pot, boil eggs in water for 10 minutes rapidly, let cool, peel and dice. Chop onion very small.
2. In a medium bowl mix all ingredients together pertaining to each salad.
3. Refrigerate and serve cold. Enjoy!

POTATO SALAD

4 SERVINGS   30 MINUTES

INGREDIENTS

3 lbs Russet Potatoes (peeled and diced)

3 Eggs (boiled)

1/2 Cup Yellow Onion (diced small)

3 Celery Stalks (chopped)

1/2 Cup Sweet Relish

2 Cups Mayonnaise

1 tsp **MKTY PERFECT S&P BLEND**

2 Tbsp Vinegar

2 Tbsp Sugar

DIRECTIONS

1. In a pot, boil peeled potatoes in lightly salted water until soft.
2. Boil eggs for 10 minutes rapidly, let cool, peel and dice. Chop onion and celery very small.
3. In a medium bowl mix all ingredients together.
4. Refrigerate and serve cold. Enjoy!

EGGS OVER STEAK &
POTATOES

SERVE AS A MEAL

4 SERVINGS   30 MINUTES

INGREDIENTS

2 lbs Ribeye Steaks

6 small Russet Potatoes

1/2 Cup Vegetable Oil

2 tbsp **MKTY PERFECT S&P BLEND**

8 Eggs

DIRECTIONS

PREHEAT OVEN TO 350°

1. Peel potatoes and dice into cubes. Place potatoes on a baking sheet and add ¼ cup oil, and season with MKTY Salt & Pepper Blend. Bake at 350 degrees for 30 minutes.

2. In a skillet, add ¼ cup oil. Season steak with MKTY S&P Blend and sear on both sides for 5 to 7 minutes, twice or until medium rare. Remove and slice into pieces.

3. Add potatoes and steak to the skillet. Mix well.

4. In another skillet, fry eggs the way you prefer and serve over steak and potatoes. Enjoy!

MKTY
PORK BLEND

.The perfect blend of spices to enhance any pork dish to bring out its delicious flavor. You are going to love it.

STUFFED MUSHROOMS &
BACON WRAPPED
JALAPENOS

4 SERVINGS   30 MINUTES

INGREDIENTS

2 lb Mushrooms
1 lb Ground Pork Sausage
1 Bunch of Green Onions
(chopped fine)
4 Garlic Cloves (crushed)
2 Tbsp **MKTY PORK BLEND**
Bread Crumbs (sprinkle)
16 oz Cream Cheese
1 Cup Parmesan Cheese
1 Egg

BACON WRAPPED JALAPENOS
RECIPE
12 Jalapenos
12 Slices of Bacon

DIRECTIONS

PREHEAT OVEN TO 350°

1. Remove stems from mushrooms and dice them
up and mix with ground pork sausage, garlic,
onion and MKTY Pork Blend. Cook until the meat
is brown. Drain and set aside.

2. Filling: In a bowl mix cream cheese, eggs, and
parmesan cheese until well blended. Then add to
the meat mixture with bread crumbs.

3. Line the mushrooms on a baking sheet and fill
each mushroom with filling. Bake for 30 minutes
at 350 degrees. Enjoy!

Bacon Wrapped Jalapeños Directions

1. Slit Jalapenos and remove seeds and stuff with
the same filling above and wrap with bacon.
Close with a toothpick and bake at 350 degrees
for 30 minutes or until bacon is crispy. Enjoy!

BRUSSEL SPROUTS, BACON & ONIONS

SERVE WITH STEAK AND RICE

4 SERVINGS   30 MINUTES

INGREDIENTS

2 lbs Brussel Sprouts (rinse and cut in half)

1 lb Bacon (chopped)

1 Medium Onion (chopped)

3 Tbsp **MKTY PORK BLEND**

2 Tbsp Olive Oil

DIRECTIONS

PREHEAT OVEN TO 350°

1. In a skillet, fry the bacon until crispy, remove from the pan and drain. Add onions and cook until caramelized. Set aside.
2. On a greased baking sheet arrange Brussel sprouts and season with MKTY Pork Blend. Bake at 350 degrees for 30 minutes or until tender.
3. Drain and mix in bacon and onions. Bake for another 10 minutes. Enjoy!

PORK FRIED RICE

SERVE WITH A GARDEN SALAD

4 SERVINGS   45 MINUTES

INGREDIENTS

2 Cups Jasmine Rice

4 Cups Water

3 Pork Steaks (chopped)

2 Tbsp **MKTY PORK BLEND**

2 Cups Cabbage (chopped)

1/2 Red Bell pepper (diced)

1/2 Green Bell Peppers (diced)

1 Cup Carrots (shredded)

4 Garlic Cloves (crushed)

2 Tbsp Soy Sauce

DIRECTIONS

1. In a pot cook rice on low heat for 30 minutes or until soft and fluffy. Let cool.

2. In a skillet, season pork chops with MKTY Pork Blend and grill for 5 to 7 minutes on each side, twice or until no longer pink. Remove and chop into cubes.

3. In a pan, sauté vegetables for 10 minutes. Add rice and pork cubes and season with MKTY Pork Blend and Soy Sauce. Enjoy!

TERIYAKI **PORK CHOP**

4 SERVINGS   30 MINUTES

INGREDIENTS

4 Thin Pork Chops
2 Tbsp **MKTY PORK BLEND**
1 Tbsp Oil

TERIYAKI SAUCE
1/2 Cup Soy Sauce
2 Tbsp Brown Sugar
4 Tbsp Water
1 Tbsp **MKTY ASIAN BLEND**

DIRECTIONS

1. Teriyaki Sauce: In a saucepan combine all the ingredients and cook slowly and stir constantly until thickened.
2. In a hot skillet, season thin pork chops with MKTY Pork Blend and grill on both sides for 5 to 7 minutes, twice or until no longer pink.
3. Base pork chops with teriyaki sauce and garnish with green onions. Enjoy!

PORK TENDERLOINS

SERVE WITH RICE PILAF

4 SERVINGS   30 MINUTES

INGREDIENTS

2 Small Pork Tenderloins
4 Tbsp Olive Oil
2 Tbsp **MKTY PORK BLEND**

SAUCE
1/2 Cup Honey
1 Tbsp Sriracha
3 Tbsp Soy Sauce
1 Tbsp Dijon Mustard

DIRECTIONS

PREHEAT OVEN TO 350°

1. Sauce: In a saucepan, mix all ingredients for the sauce together and cook on low for 10 minutes.
2. In a skillet, add oil and seasoned pork tenderloins. Sear on all sides for about 3 to 5 minutes per side.
3. Add tenderloins to a roasting pan, cover with foil and bake at 350° for 45 minutes. Remove foil and base tenderloins with sauce and bake for another 15 minutes. The last 5 minutes, base with sauce and set the oven to broil for 3-5 minutes to give that charbroil appearance. Allow tenderloins to cool, slice, and enjoy!

MKTY
SPICY BLEND

Spicy! But not so much that you can't enjoy it. It has just the right amount of heat. You are going to love it.

SPICY **CHICKEN SANDWICH**

4 SERVINGS   30 MINUTES

INGREDIENTS

4 Chicken Breast (boneless and butterfly)
1 Cup Flour
2 Tbsp **MKTY SPICY BLEND**
1/2 Cup Vegetable Oil
Lettuce
2 Tomatoes (sliced)
1/2 Red Onion (Sliced)
Mayonnaise
Mustard
4 Hamburger Buns

DIRECTIONS

1. Season butterflied chicken breast with MKTY Spicy Blend. Dredge in flour, shake off excess flour.
2. In a hot skillet add oil and fry chicken on both sides for 5 to 7 minutes each side, twice or until golden brown and well done on the inside.
3. Start building your spicy chicken sandwich. Toppings are optional. Enjoy!

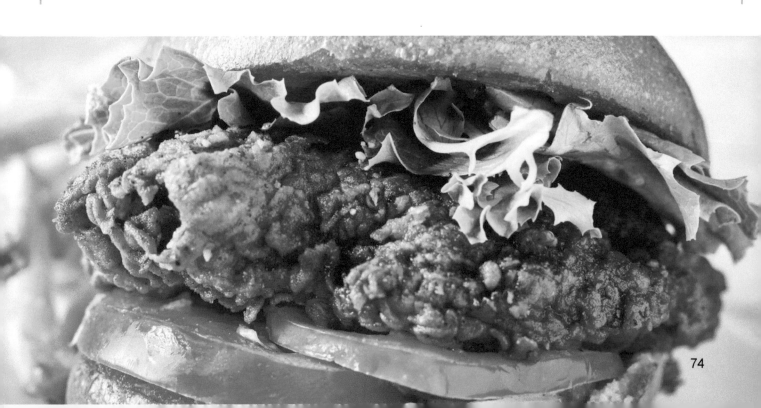

SPICY BLACKENED
SALMON

SERVE WITH GARLIC HERB
BUTTER RICE

4 SERVINGS   30 MINUTES

INGREDIENTS

2 lbs Salmon
1 Tbsp **MKTY SPICY BLEND**
2 Tbsp Olive Oil

DIRECTIONS

1. Cut Salmon into steak size portions and season with MKTY Spicy Blend.
2. In a hot skillet, grill salmon on both sides for 4 to 5 minutes, twice until it is no longer translucent pink.
3. Serve over a bed of garlic herb butter rice. Enjoy

SPICY **CHICKEN GOULASH**

4 SERVINGS   30 MINUTES

INGREDIENTS

3 Chicken Breast (cubed)
1 Tbsp **MKTY SPICY BLEND***
1/4 Cup Vegetable Oil
16 oz Can of Corn (drained)
16 oz Can of Diced Tomatoes
(drained)
3 Zucchini (diced)
2 Yellow Squash (diced)
1 Bunch Cilantro (chopped)
Sprinkle Parmesan cheese

DIRECTIONS

1. Chop the chicken breast into cubes and season with MKTY Spicy Blend.
2. In a hot skillet, add oil and blacken chicken for 5 to 7 minutes on both sides, twice or until golden brown.
3. Remove, chop and set aside.
4. In the same skillet, add zucchini, squash corn, tomatoes and cilantro and cook for 10 minutes longer, add blackened chicken. Garnish with parmesan cheese. Enjoy!

Can be substituted with MKTY Blend

SPICY **POTATOES**

SERVE AS A SIDE

4 SERVINGS   40 MINUTES

INGREDIENTS

6 Large Russet Potatoes (cubed)
1/2 Cup Vegetable Oil
1 Tbsp **MKTY SPICY BLEND**

DIRECTIONS

<u>PREHEAT OVEN TO 350°</u>

1. Rinse, peel and cube potatoes. Place on a baking sheet, drizzle with oil and season with MKTY Spicy Blend.
2. Bake at 350 degrees for 40 minutes or until crispy. Enjoy!

SPICY FRIED
CHICKEN/TENDERS

SERVE WITH MAC-N-CHEESE AND GREEN BEANS

4 SERVINGS   30 MINUTES

INGREDIENTS

3 lbs Chicken (cut up)
2 Cups of Self-Rising Flour
4 TBSP **MKTY SPICY BLEND**
3 Cup Vegetable Oil

DIRECTIONS

1. In a bowl with a lid, season the chicken with 3 Tbsp MKTY Spicy Blend and let it sit in the refrigerator for 4 hours or overnight.
2. In another bowl with a lid, add flour with 1 TBSP MKTY Spicy Blend, add chicken close lid and shake off excess flour.
3. In a skillet, add oil and fry for chicken 8-10 minutes on each side, twice or until golden brown or reaches 180° internal temperature.
4. Remove chicken from the frying pan and place on a paper towel to drain excess oil. Enjoy!

Or spray chicken heavily with pam cooking spray, add chicken to the air fryer for 15 minutes minutes at 400° and then flip and cook for an additional 15 minutes more.

SPICY **ASPARAGUS PASTA**

SERVE WITH A GREEN SALAD

4 SERVINGS   30 MINUTES

INGREDIENTS

1 Stalk Fresh Asparagus (cut in half)
1/2 Box Penne Pasta
1 Cup Cherry Tomatoes
1 Bag Spinach

DRESSING
Sprinkle **MKTY SPICY BLEND**
2 Tbsp Olive Oil
1/4 Cup Red Vinegar

DIRECTIONS

1. Cook pasta according to instructions on the package.
2. Dressing: Add all ingredients into a bowl and whisk together
3. In a pan sauté the asparagus for about 10 minutes. Add tomatoes and spinach last 5 minutes.
4. In a large bowl mix pasta, vegetables, and dressing Sprinkle on MKTY Spicy Blend. Enjoy!

Can serve cold or hot

SPICY **PINEAPPLE STEAK**

4 SERVINGS   30 MINUTES

INGREDIENTS

2 lbs Sirloin Steak (cut up)

1 Tbsp **MKTY SPICY BLEND**

2 Tbsp Olive Oil

1 Red Bell Pepper (chunks)

1 Green Bell Peppers (chunks)

1 Yellow Onion (cubes)

5 Garlic Cloves (crushed)

16 oz Can Pineapple Slices (drain and save juice)

SAUCE

1/4 Cup Brown Sugar

1/2 Cup Low Sodium Soy Sauce

2 tsp Sesame Seed Oil

1 tsp **MKTY PORK BLEND**

1/2 Cup Pineapple Juice

1/4 Cup Water

1 Tbsp Cornstarch

DIRECTIONS

1. Sauce: In a saucepan mix brown sugar, soy sauce, sesame oil, MKTY Pork Blend, pineapple juice, water and cornstarch. Cook on low and stir until thickened.
2. In a skillet lightly sauté bell peppers and onions in oil. Remove from the skillet.
3. In the same skillet add oil and season cut up steak with MKTY Spicy Blend, and sear for 5 to 7 minutes on each side until medium-well done.
4. Add the vegetables and sauce simmer for 5 minutes. Add pineapples, simmer for 5 minutes longer. Enjoy!

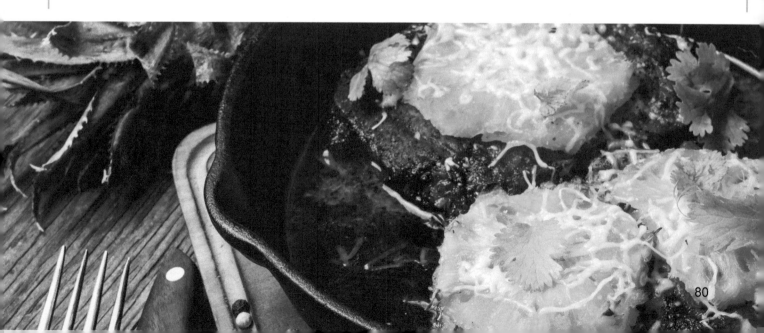

MKTY
STEAK BLEND

This Blend will awaken the flavor of any steak or beef. You are going to love it.

PERFECT STEAK

4 SERVINGS   30 MINUTES

INGREDIENTS

24 oz Sirloin Steak (or your
choice)
1 TBSP **MKTY STEAK BLEND**
1 Tbsp Butter

DIRECTIONS

1. In a cast iron skillet add butter and season steak with MKTY Steak Blend and grill on both sides for 5 to 8 minutes until medium well.

Remember it's not the recipe that gives the flavor it is the seasonings. Enjoy!

SIRLOIN **CHEESEBURGER**

SERVE WITH COLESLAW

4 SERVINGS   30 MINUTES

INGREDIENTS

1 lbs Ground Beef Sirloin*
2 Tbsp **MKTY STEAK BLEND**
1/2 head Lettuce
3 Tomato (sliced)
1 Onion (sliced)
8 slices of Cheese
1 Pack of Hamburger Buns

SAUCE
2 Tbsp Mayo
1 Tbsp Worcestershire Sauce
1 Tbsp Barbecue sauce (recipe is
on page 25 in the book)

DIRECTIONS

1. Sauce: In a bowl, mix all the ingredients well.
2. Season sirloin with MKTY Steak Blend and form patties. Place patties on a grill or in a pan, and cook until medium well. Cook 5 to 7 minutes on both sides, twice. until medium well.
3. Start building your burger as follows: bun, sauce, lettuce, tomato, patty, Cheese, onionTomatoes, Onions, end with sauce on top of the bun. Enjoy!

Can substitute for Impossible meat or ground turkey

TENDER **ROAST BEEF**

4 SERVINGS   120 MINUTES

INGREDIENTS

3 lbs Pot Roast
2 Tbsp Olive Oil
3 Celery Stalk
4 Potatoes (cut up)
3 Large Carrots (cut up)
2 Small Onion
6 Garlic cloves (chopped)
3 Tbsp **MKTY STEAK BLEND**
1/4 Cup Worcestershire sauce
1/2 Cup Water

DIRECTIONS

PREHEAT OVEN TO 350°

1. In a skillet add oil and brown Roast for 5 minutes on all sides.
2. In a roasting pan add rinsed and cut vegetables, along with the roast and season with MKTY Steak Blend and Worcestershire sauce.
3. Bake at 350 degrees, cover and walk away for 2 1/2 hours, uncover and cook for 30 minutes more. Enjoy!

STEAK & BROCCOLI

SERVE WITH STEAMED RICE

4 SERVINGS   30 MINUTES

INGREDIENTS

2 lb Flank Steak
5 cups Broccoli (florets)
3 Tbsp **MKTY STEAK BLEND**
1/2 Cup Low -Sodium Soy sauce
4 Tbsp Butter

DIRECTIONS

1. Rinse and cut up Broccoli, set aside.
2. Cut Steak into slices, season with MKTY Steak Blend.
3. In a hot skillet add butter and sear steaks for 5 minutes on both sides, or until medium well. Remove from the skillet.
4. Add Broccoli and a pinch of MKTY Steak Blend. Cook for 10 minutes or until broccoli is soft add low sodium soy sauce and steak. Enjoy!

NOT YOUR ORDINARY "ASPARAGUS"

SERVE AS A MEAL OR WITH YOUR CHOICE OF MEAT

4 SERVINGS   30 MINUTES

INGREDIENTS

1/2 lb Bacon (thinly sliced)
2 lbs Asparagus
4 Tbsp Garlic Butter
1 Tbsp **MKTY STEAK BLEND**
1/4 Cup Parmesan Cheese

GARLIC BUTTER
1 Stick of Butter (soft)
8 Garlic cloves (boiled)
1 Cup Water

DIRECTIONS

PREHEAT OVEN TO 350°

1. Garlic Butter: In a small saucepan, add water and garlic. Boil until the garlic is soft. Remove and blend into butter.
2. Lay asparagus onto a baking pan and brush with garlic butter.
3. Bundle asparagus into fours, wrap with a piece of bacon and season with MKTY Steak Blend.
4. Bake at 350 degrees for 30 minutes or until bacon is cooked. Sprinkle with Parmesan cheese. Enjoy!

TENDER BEEF TIPS & GRAVY

4 SERVINGS   90 MINUTES

INGREDIENTS

2 lbs Sirloin Beef Tips
3 Tbsp Flour
3 Tbsp Olive Oil
3 Tbsp **MKTY STEAK BLEND**

GRAVY
3 Tbsp Vegetable Oil
3 Tbsp Flour
2 Cup Mushrooms (sliced)
2 cups Low Sodium Beef Broth
2 Tbsp **MKTY STEAK BLEND**
2 tsp Worcestershire Sauce
1/4 Cup Water

DIRECTIONS

PREHEAT OVEN TO 350°

1. Gravy: In a skillet, add oil and brown the flour. Add beef broth and whisk until smooth. Add mushrooms and simmer until mushrooms are tender. Season gravy with MKTY Steak blend, Worcestershire sauce. Cook on low until thickened.
2. Season Sirloin Tips with MKTY Steak Blend and dust in flour.
3. In a hot skillet, add oil and sear until golden brown on all sides. Remove from the skillet.
4. Add Sirloin Tips to the gravy, cover and bake at 350 degrees for an 1 1/2 hours or until super tender. Enjoy!

MKTY
TACO BLEND

This delicious blend is not just for tacos. This spice enhances the flavor of any Mexican dish. You are going to love it.

MEXICAN **PIZZA**

4 SERVINGS   60 MINUTES

INGREDIENTS

1 lb Ground Beef*
1/2 Onion (diced)
1/2 Green Bell Pepper (diced)
4 Garlic Cloves (crushed)
16 oz Tomato Sauce
16 oz Can Refried Beans
3 Cups Taco Blend Cheese
2 Cups Mozzarella cheese
2 Tbsp **MKTY TACO BLEND**
16 Small Flour Tortillas
1/2 Cup Vegetable Oil

DIRECTIONS

1. In a skillet, add the ground beef, onion, bell pepper, garlic, tomato sauce and MKTY Taco Blend. Cook on medium heat until the meat is brown. Remove from the pan.
2. In a clean skillet fry tortillas golden brown. And set aside.
3. Prepare pizza with a shell on the bottom, beans, meat sauce, cheese and another shell on top, ending with meat sauce and cheese. Garnish with green onions. Enjoy!

Can substitute for Impossible meat or ground turkey

89

BEEF **FAJITAS**

SERVE WITH CILANTRO LIME
RICE

4 SERVINGS   30 MINUTES

INGREDIENTS

20 oz Flank or Ribeye Steaks*
4 Tbsp Olive Oil
2 Medium white onion
1 Red bell pepper
1 Yellow bell pepper
1 Large Poblano Pepper (optional)
1/2 Cup Cilantro (garnish)
Sour cream
Shredded cheese
Guacamole
2 Limes (cut into quarters)
8 Flour or corn Tortillas

MARINADE
1 Tbsp **MKTY TACO BLEND**
1/3 Cup Lime Juice
2 Tbsp Worcestershire Sauce
3 Tbsp Olive Oil

DIRECTIONS

1. Marinade: Mix all ingredients together and and marinade steak overnight.
2. Slice onions and bell peppers julienne style (ahead of time)
3. In a large cast iron skillet add olive oil and sear marinated meat for 5 minutes on each side or until medium rare. Remove meat and slice.
4. Add olive oil to the same skillet, sauté the vegetables and season with MKTY Taco Blend.
5. Add the meat to the vegetables and begin filling warmed tortillas with meat and vegetables, and serve with Sour Cream, Guacamole, cheese, lime and garnish with cilantro. Enjoy!

*Can substitute for chicken breast

CHICKEN **TACOS**

SERVE WITH RICE AND BEANS

4 SERVINGS   30 MINUTES

INGREDIENTS

4 Chicken Breast*
2 TBSP **MKTY TACO BLEND**
2 Tbsp Olive Oil
1 Bag of Cole Slaw
12 Tortillas

AVOCADO SALSA
1 Cup Mayonnaise
1/2 Bunch Cilantro (chopped)
1/2 Jalapeno (seedless)
1/4 Cup Avocado Oil
4 Garlic
1 TBSP **MKTY PERFECT S&P BLEND**

DIRECTIONS

1. Avocado Salsa: In a Nutri-bullet or blender add mayonnaise, cilantro, avocado oil, garlic, jalapeno and MKTY S&P Blend. Blend until smooth.
2. In a skillet, add oil and Season Chicken Breast with MKTY Taco and sear for 5 to 7 minutes, on both sides, twice or no longer pink. Shred chicken and set aside.
3. Lightly fry shells in olive oil and then fill with meat and Cole slaw, drizzle Sauce on top. Enjoy!

Can substitute for ground beef or ground turkey

TURKEY **ENCHILADAS**

SERVE WITH RICE AND BEANS

4 SERVINGS   30 MINUTES

INGREDIENTS

1 lb Ground Turkey*
1/2 Yellow Onion (chopped)
6 Garlic Cloves (crushed)
2 Tbsp **MKTY TACO BLEND**
3 Cups Mexican Cheese Blend
12 Corn Tortilla
3 Tbsp Vegetable Oil

ENCHILADA SAUCE
4 Tbsp Butter
4 Tbsp Flour
14.5 oz. Crushed Tomatoes
8 oz Tomato Sauce
3 Tbsp **MKTY TACO BLEND**
15 oz Chicken Broth

DIRECTIONS

PREHEAT OVEN TO 350°

1. Enchilada Sauce: In a pot on low, melt butter and stir in flour, add chicken broth whisk until smooth and season with MKTY Taco Blend, add crushed Tomatoes and tomato sauce. Cook on low for 20 minutes. Set aside.

2. In a skillet add ground Turkey, onions, Bell Peppers and MKTY Taco Blend. Cook until the meat is brown.

3. In a skillet, lightly fry tortillas shells for 30 seconds, then dip each shell in the Enchilada sauce and fill each shell with meat and cheese.

4. Arrange in a 6 X 9 pan and pour the remaining sauce over the shells and sprinkle with cheese. Bake at 350 degrees for 20 minutes until the cheese is melted. Enjoy!

Can be substituted with ground beef or Impossible Meat

TACO SALAD

4 SERVINGS   30 MINUTES

INGREDIENTS

1 lb Ground Turkey*
32 oz Can Pinto Beans (optional)
2 Tbsp **MKTY TACO BLEND**
1/2 Head of Lettuce (shredded)
2 Tomato (diced)
1 Green Onions
1 Large Bag Favorite Doritos
2 Cups Cheese (shredded)
Thousand Island Dressing or
Avocado Salsa

DIRECTIONS

1. In a skillet, season ground turkey with MKTY Taco Blend and cook until browned, drain and add pinto beans.
2. Chop lettuce, dice tomatoes and onions and mix all together.
3. Layer on a plate in this order, Doritos, meat mixture, vegetables and top with cheese and dressing. Or mix everything together in a bowl. Enjoy!

Can be substituted with ground beef or Impossible Meat.

MKTY STREET **TACOS**

4 SERVINGS   30 MINUTES

INGREDIENTS

20 oz Ribeyes (chopped)
1 Tbsp **MKTY TACO BLEND**
24 mini Corn Tortillas
1/4 Cup Vegetable Oil
1/2 Onion
1 bunch cilantro (chopped)

AVOCADO SALSA
1 Cup Mayonnaise
1/2 Bunch Cilantro (chopped)
1/2 Jalapeno (seedless)
1/4 Cup Avocado Oil
4 Garlic
1 TBSP **MKTY PERFECT S&P BLEND**

DIRECTIONS

1. Avocado Salsa: Mix all the ingredients in a Nutri-bullet or blender and blend well.
2. In a skillet, season steak with MKTY Taco Blend and sear on both sides for 5 to 6 minutes, or cook until medium well. Chop small and set aside.
3. Heat the oil on medium heat and fry tortillas softly.
4. double the tortillas and fill tortilla shells with steak and garnish with onions and cilantro. Drizzle with Avocado dressing. Enjoy!

MY! MY! MY! TACO PIE

4 SERVINGS   30 MINUTES

INGREDIENTS

1 lbs Ground Beef*

2 Tbsp **MKTY TACO BLEND**

1/2 Onion

4 Garlic Cloves (crush)

16 oz Can Tomato sauce

1 Head lettuce (shredded)

3 Tomato (diced)

1 Green Onions (chopped)

Sour Cream

2 ½ Cups Cheddar Cheese

18 Tortillas Shells

DIRECTIONS

PREHEAT OVEN TO 350°

1. In a skillet brown the ground beef with onion, garlic, tomato sauce and season with MKTY Taco Blend. Cook until no longer pink.

2. In a 9 x 13 baking pan begin to layer starting with meat sauce, then 6 tortillas, meat sauce, cheese, 6 tortillas, meat sauce, cheese, 6 tortillas, meat sauce, cheese.

3. Bake at 350 degrees for 30 minutes.

4. Remove from the oven and let cool for 10 minutes. Top with lettuce, tomatoes, sour cream and green onions. Enjoy!

Can be substituted with ground Turkey or Impossible Meat.

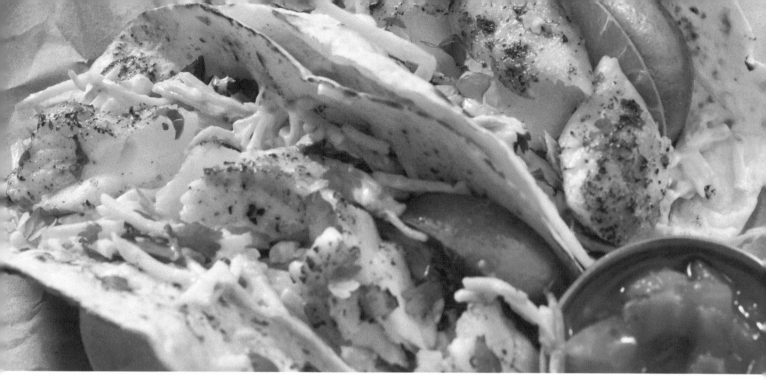

OMG! FISH TACOS

SERVE WITH BEANS AND RICE

4 SERVINGS   30 MINUTES

INGREDIENTS

6 Tilapia (filet)

4 Tbsp Butter

2 Tbsp **MKTY TACO BLEND**

8 Flour Tortillas

1 Small Onion (diced)

1 bag of Cole Slaw

2 Limes (cut in quarters)

AVOCADO SALSA

1 Cup Mayonnaise

1/2 Bunch Cilantro (chopped)

1 Jalapeno (seedless)

1/4 Cup Avocado Oil

4 Garlic

1 TBSP **MKTY PERFECT S&P BLEND**

DIRECTIONS

1. Avocado Salsa: Mix all the ingredients in a Nutri-bullet or blender and blend well.

2. In a skillet, add butter and sauté ½ of the onions for 10 minutes. Remove onions. Add seasoned Tilapia and cook until no longer translucent, flake apart the Tilapia with a fork and add onions back to the skillet.

3. In a clean skillet add oil and fry the tortilla shell softly. Fill the shells with blackened Tilapia. Garnish with Cole slaw and lime. Top off with the Avocado Salsa. Enjoy!

NOTES

NOTES

NOTES

NOTES

CPSIA information can be obtained
at www.ICGtesting.com
Printed in the USA
LVHW072334290822
727115LV00009B/129